Original title:
Candies, Carols, and Christmas Cheer

Copyright © 2024 Creative Arts Management OÜ
All rights reserved.

Author: Dexter Sullivan
ISBN HARDBACK: 978-9916-90-872-3
ISBN PAPERBACK: 978-9916-90-873-0

Frosted Wishes and Twinkling Lights

In a world of frosted dreams,
The laughter echoes through the beams.
Little elves in jolly hats,
Dancing round with talking cats.

Baking cookies, what a sight,
Flour fights and frosted bites.
Sprinkles flying, icing wars,
Who knew sweet would open doors?

We sing loud with silly glee,
Rhymes that make no sense, you see.
Lights that twinkle, twirl, and spin,
Spread the giggles, let the fun begin!

Sugar-Plum Harmonies

A jolly feast of sugar smiles,
Giggling through the snowy miles.
Every song we belt and croon,
Tastes just like a giant balloon.

Tiny reindeer stomp and play,
While sugar fairies pass the day.
Sweet potato with marshmallow glow,
Laugh until we spill the dough.

The tunes are silly, just like pies,
Glitter in the children's eyes.
With every note, chaos erupts,
Sugar dreams and giggles, we disrupt!

The Joy of Frosted Delights

With frosting thick upon the cake,
Every bite's a joyful shake.
Laughter bubbles, giggles burst,
In the land where sweets come first.

Chocolates wearing silly hats,
Taffy tangled in the mats.
All around the joy we share,
In this silly, frosted fair.

Jingle bells and giggles round,
Funny faces all around.
With every treat, a loud cheer sings,
For the joy that sweetness brings!

Melodies Beneath the Mistletoe

Underneath the leafy mist,
Kissing candy with a twist.
Everyone is feeling grand,
As we share a goofy band.

Bouncing, laughing, what a show,
Silly hats, and mischief flow.
Lollipop sticks held up high,
Throwing whispers to the sky.

Cocoa mugs and marshmallow hugs,
Jolly jokes that need no plugs.
Let's create a tale so bright,
With melodies that twinkle light!

Glimmering Spirits of Togetherness

Jingle bells in muddy boots,
Laughter sprouts like silly roots.
Grandma did a dance, oh dear,
Spilled the punch and lost her cheer.

Uncle Joe with eggnog breath,
Tells strange tales that flirt with death.
A cat in lights, a dog in bows,
This festive chaos surely grows.

Tastes of Home and Heart

Cookies shaped like bizarre trees,
Frosting fights with sticky knees.
Grandpa's secret five- bean stew,
Just what we need, or maybe not, too.

Chocolates stuck to every chair,
Whipped cream blobs are everywhere.
A taste of love, a dash of spice,
Every single bite is twice as nice.

Nightingale Nibbles and Yuletide Bliss

Singing songs with funny notes,
Niblings dance in odd-shaped coats.
A pie that wiggles, wobbles, rolls,
And tickles everyone's sweet souls.

Mistletoe placed on dog's right ear,
Is it a kiss or just a cheer?
Laughter rings, a gift of fun,
Joyful chaos for everyone.

Warmth in Every Hug

Hugs that squeeze like jellybeans,
Giggles burst at awkward scenes.
Every grin a cozy spark,
Even when it gets too dark.

Cousins plotting prankish schemes,
Silly laughter floods our dreams.
With warm embraces, love will flow,
In this delight, our spirits grow.

Sweet Serenades of the Season

Gummy bears jingling in the night,
Frolicking elves with marzipan delight.
Lollipops dancing, oh what a sight,
Sugar-sweet laughter, the mood feels just right.

Chocolates waltzing under twinkling lights,
Candy canes prancing, as joy ignites.
Sprinkles of giggles and fruity bites,
Smiles like fireworks, soaring to new heights.

Melodies Wrapped in Frosted Dreams

Fudge so rich it sings a tune,
Dreamy marshmallows float like a balloon.
Brittle laughter breaks out at noon,
Cookies gossip 'neath the silver moon.

Caramel drizzles on a snow-white hill,
Sugar rush poetry that gives a thrill.
Sweets in baskets, everyone pays the bill,
With each little nibble, the heart finds its will.

Twinkling Treats in Winter's Embrace

Lemon drops chasing the frosty air,
Chubby gumdrops filled with flair.
Frosting snowmen with frosting to spare,
Jelly beans giggle without a care.

Nuts and bolts made of crunchy bliss,
A gingerbread frog giving a kiss.
With every bite, we share a wish,
Holiday giggles wrapped up in this.

Sugarplum Symphony on Starry Nights

Cotton candy clouds float so high,
Marshmallow moons in the chocolate sky.
Jolly tunes and a sprightly sigh,
A candy parade, oh my, oh my!

Licorice laughter fills the fray,
Rainbow sprinkles brighten the day.
Peanut brittle at a grand buffet,
In this sweet wonderland, we all want to stay.

Surprises Hidden in Layers of Light

In wrappings bright and shiny,
Tiny treasures wait inside,
Like a squirrel that found a nut,
Giggles echo, joy and pride.

When the paper starts to tear,
It's a peek at what's to be,
A fuzzy sock or rubber duck,
Oh, what will the next gift see?

Home Away from Home

Gather round, it's time to feast,
With loud laughter and a roar,
From the kitchen wafts a smell,
Like cookies baked, we all implore.

Cards and games, a wild night,
With slippery floors and sliding feet,
Slapstick falls, we burst with glee,
As we dance to our own beat.

Joy in Every Glimpse of Snow

Fluffy flakes like cotton candy,
Swirl and twirl in the evening glow,
We gather, laughing, not too fancy,
Creating mischief in the snow.

Snowballs flying, a playful fight,
How they splat with squeaks and squeals,
Every toss a giggling delight,
Laughter fills the air, it heals.

The Spirit of Solstice and Harmony

A wobbly dance under moon's light,
With friends that shine as bright as day,
We sway like trees in gentle air,
With silly moves, we laugh and play.

Voices raise in joyous tune,
Off-key notes that jingle well,
Our hearts wrapped in warm cocoon,
In this moment, we all dwell.

Flavors of Joy in the Chill of Night

In the frost a sweet delight,
Chasing giggles through the night,
Lollipops in snowflakes twirl,
While grinning faces dance and whirl.

Hot cocoa spills, a marshmallow mess,
Sipping joy in pure excess,
Gummy bears with frosty hats,
Mischief hides beneath the mats.

Merrymaking Beneath the Evergreen

Beneath the tree, we jump and play,
Twinkling lights lead the way,
A candy cane army in the fight,
Caroling squirrels in party light.

Pinecones join in the fun,
Making mischief, everyone,
Jelly beans fight for a taste,
In laughter, not a moment to waste.

Whispers of Warmth in a World of Cold

Beneath blankets, cozy and wide,
Hot treats trying to hide,
With giggles echoing in the chill,
Laughter builds like a giant hill.

Fuzzy socks and peppermint dreams,
Silly hats burst at the seams,
Snowmen wearing our granddad's tie,
Fun just melting, oh my, oh my!

Whirlygigs and Sugar Dreams

Round and round the merry-go,
Candy laughter starts to flow,
Spinning tops and sugary charms,
Wrapped in giggles, safe from harms.

Sundae hats atop our heads,
Popcorn trails leading to beds,
With every swirl our hearts take flight,
Dancing stars in the whimsical night.

Beneath the Stars of Family Ties

Under the twinkling twilight glow,
Uncles dance like they've lost their toe.
Aunties giggle as they spill the punch,
Cousins huddle to munch and crunch.

Grandma's sweater, it's quite the sight,
Made the cat look ready to bite.
Jokes and jests fly through the air,
Laughter bounces without a care.

Enchantment Under a Skating Sky

Skates go flying, someone takes a fall,
Hot cocoa spills, but it's still a ball!
Snowflakes twirl like socks in a spin,
Watch your step, oh dear, don't fall in!

Children giggle as they slide on ice,
Mittens clash—oh, isn't it nice?
A bumpy ride on shovels galore,
Gloves so wet, we laugh and roar.

Mellow Moments by the Firelight

The fire crackles, the marshmallows burn,
Dad's dad jokes make the kids all squirm.
Siblings tease, who toasted the best?
It's a wild game of who steals the zest!

Pajamas are fuzzy, socks mismatched,
Melted dreams, where sweet talks are hatched.
Ghost stories creep, with spooky delight,
We snicker and squeal, through the long night.

Wishes Adrift in the Fresh Air

Outside the door, the snowflakes gleam,
Kids chasing dreams, or so it would seem.
Wish lists tossed like papers in flight,
Giggles echo, what a silly sight!

Footprints skate through the powdery fluff,
"We need more snacks, this isn't enough!"
Caught in a snowball, twice a row,
Wishes whirled like flurries in tow.

Laughing Shadows and Glittering Hopes

In the corner, a snowman grins,
With a carrot nose, it surely wins.
A cheeky elf does a silly dance,
Spreading laughter at every chance.

Jingle bells ring with a clumsy sound,
As clowns in bright colors tumble around.
Tinsel tangled in a giggling spree,
Oh, the chaos of this festive glee!

Sugarplums bounce on the floor, I swear,
While reindeer battle, flying through the air.
A puppy pounces, catching the light,
As confetti rains down, oh, what a sight!

With hopscotch lights upon the tree,
We toast to laughs in jubilee.
As shadows dance with frosty cheer,
We relish the warmth of the season near.

Midnight Magic in a Snowy Veil

Under twinkling stars, a cat takes flight,
Chasing shadows in the chilly night.
A snowball fight, oh what a mess,
But giggles echo, we're feeling blessed.

Pinecones juggling, they don't stand still,
As the moonlight bathes us in a thrill.
A chorus of snickers fills the air,
While chocolate sprinkles dance without a care.

With socks that match in dazzling hues,
And crumpets served, oh, such a muse!
Gingerbread men skip on the floor,
Their frosting smiles making us roar.

Amidst this night, where laughter thrums,
We raise our mugs, oh, how fun it hums!
In the frosty glow, our spirits soar,
As midnight magic keeps us wanting more.

Sweets of Solstice Dancing in the Air

In the kitchen, sugar flies,
Flour clouds, a sweet surprise!
Gumdrops bounce from here to there,
As giggles fill the frosty air.

Mixing bowls, they swirl and spin,
Sprinkles dance, let the fun begin!
Lollipops join in the fray,
While frosting fights the day away.

Baking chaos, flour on my nose,
Candied chaos, who knows how it goes?
But laughter echoes, sweetening the day,
With wishes for fun in every way.

From oven warmth to frosty night,
Sugarplum dreams, oh what a sight!
Dancing shadows, playful delight,
As joy cascades into the night.

Joyful Rhythms of Holiday Tidings

Jingle bells toss through the air,
Tinsel trails without a care!
Sipping cocoa, laughter flows,
Sneaky snacks in every pose.

Chorus of chuckles, voices sing,
Merry moments that joy will bring!
Elves in hiding share a wink,
While we all dive in to drink.

Confetti snowflakes whirl around,
As friends unite on joyful ground.
Ticklish toes and chocolate bites,
Equal merriment on chilly nights.

Under the lights, we strut and sway,
Lost in fun until the day.
With silly hats and ginger glee,
We'll dance forever, just you and me.

The Enchanted Feast of Tranquil Nights

Under stars, we gather tight,
With treats that glimmer in the night.
Plates piled high with bites so sweet,
As laughter dances with our feet.

Cheesy smiles and faces bright,
As marshmallow floats take flight!
Talking bears and cookie dreams,
All mixed up in giggly schemes.

Muffins giggle, cakes take a bow,
Who knew sweets could cause a row?
With each snack, a joke unfurls,
As friends unite in creamy swirls.

The moonlight sparkles on our treats,
Filling hearts and stomping beats.
In cozy nooks, we spread good cheer,
With whispered secrets all night near.

Whimsical Wonders Wrapped in Ribbon

Presents piled with bows and cheer,
Wrapped up tight, the end is near!
Fingers sticky with the tape,
As we giggle and start to gape.

Fuzzy socks and goofy hats,
Underfoot, a cat that sat.
Ribbons twirl, a tangled string,
As we dance and laugh and cling.

Delivery trucks with candy loads,
Make our silly hearts explode!
Box after box, our joy is free,
In this festive, wacky spree.

The magic sparkles in the air,
As folks unwrap with cheerful flair.
And in the chaos, love appears,
Laughter rained down through all the years.

Tinsel Tunes and Cocoa Mugs

Jingle bells clatter, oh what a sight,
A cat in a scarf, trying to take flight.
Marshmallows floating in mugs so round,
A snowman with mittens, he just fell down!

Chocolates are melting, all gooey and bright,
Elves in the kitchen, what a wild night!
Sprinkles are flying, they dance on the floor,
We laugh till we snort, then we belly-store!

Whispers of Winter Warmth

Snowflakes are giggling, swirling in glee,
A reindeer in shades, sipping sweet tea.
Pudding that wiggles, it wants to explore,
It jumps off the table—oh wait, there's more!

Socks on the fireplace, mismatched and loud,
A hamster in plaid, he thinks he's quite proud.
Gifts wrapped in laughter, with bows gone astray,
Who wrapped the dog? Now he's part of the play!

Lullabies of the Festive Night

The moon wears a hat, it's quite absurd,
While mice sing a tune that's completely unheard.
Pinecones are playing a melody sweet,
While grandpa's off snoozing, lost in his seat.

Cookies are winking, with icing all bright,
They dodged the big cat, then danced in delight.
Laughter erupts as the snowflakes collide,
A squirrel on a sleigh now enjoys the ride!

Echoes of Starlit Joy

Stars have a giggle; they twinkle so wide,
A bear in a tutu is taking a ride.
Jugs full of jellybeans, bouncing around,
What's this? A jump scare? It's just the sound!

The night wears a grin, wrapped up in its glow,
Fairies on skis, giving soft night shows.
The air is electric, with frolicking glee,
As whispers of mischief tumble like the sea!

Songs of Giving and Glorious Dreams

In a land where sweet treats dance,
Sugar squirrels in a candy trance.
Lollipops drop from candy trees,
And marshmallow clouds float in the breeze.

Chubby elves with jingle bells,
Share their giggles and silly yells.
Bumping into gingerbread men,
Laughing, "Let's do it all again!"

Frosting frolics shine so bright,
Sprinkled sprits in pink delight.
A chorus sung with chocolate cheer,
Making joy spread far and near.

As dreams unfold in frosted dreams,
With silly songs and laughter beams.
We dance around in purest glee,
Creating magic, just you and me.

Starshine and Cozy Embrace

Under twinkling lights so bold,
Snickering stories never told.
Hot cocoa spills on winter's night,
Marshmallows fly in a sweet flight.

Warming hugs with cookie crumbs,
Ticklish toes and joyful thumbs.
As stars wink from their lofty gloom,
We burst with laughter, fill the room.

Pine trees wear a sprinkle crown,
While giggles bloom all around.
A sprinkle fight breaks out, oh fun!
We snort and laugh, our worries shun.

In cozy corners, dreams ignite,
With whispers shared and soft twilight.
Each heart wraps up in silly ways,
Finding bliss in silly plays.

Love Wrapped in Colorful Bows

Gifts wrapped tight in shiny wraps,
Crackling sounds like tiny claps.
Unraveling with shouts of glee,
Surprise! There's more than you can see.

Fuzzy socks? A wiggly toy!
Each unboxing brings such joy.
With giggles bright and hearts so warm,
Every present holds a charm.

Tangled ribbons, bows askew,
Each little package hides a clue.
A silly hat or prank-filled gift,
Sparkling laughs give spirits a lift.

In this season, hearts collide,
As laughter flows and worries slide.
Wrapped with humor, hugs, and cheer,
Creating memories year by year.

Sipping Joy Beneath the Lights

Sipping warmth from mugs so round,
Chocolate rivers swirl unbound.
With peppermint swirls on the rim,
Our giggles echo, voices brim.

Outside, the snowflakes dance with glee,
While we sip and chat, just you and me.
Spilling drinks on every side,
As laughter flows, there's nowhere to hide.

Racing snowmen with silly hats,
We trip and tumble like nimble cats.
With every cheer, and warmth we find,
Our hearts align, our spirits twined.

Beneath the stars, a sparkling show,
We sip our drinks, our faces aglow.
In this moment, the joy we stake,
As laughter fills the night we make.

Threads of Joy in a Colorful Quilt

A patchwork of laughter, stitched so tight,
Gummies and giggles dance through the night.
With sprinkles of joy, the fabric sways,
Each square holds a story of silly play.

Lollipop trees in a meadow of dreams,
Swirling like snowflakes, or so it seems.
We twirl and we spin in a whirl of delight,
Wrapped in warmth on this magical night.

Jellybean rivers that bubble and flow,
With marshmallow clouds, we giggle and glow.
Under the stars, we share silly tales,
Where laughter ignites, and joy always prevails.

Starry-Eyed Children and Shining Joy

With eyes like saucers, and hearts full of glee,
They dance 'round the tree, all covered in spree.
Whispers of mischief float up in the air,
As tinsel gets tangled in tousled hair.

Gifts wrapped in laughter, surprises galore,
Sticky-fingered giggles tumble on the floor.
Pies cooling swiftly, so late in the game,
Chasing down crumbs, oh what a silly claim!

Each moment a treasure, they stash in their minds,
Giggling like hyenas, no need for rewinds.
In the glow of the night, joy brightly beams,
Starry-eyed children weave whimsy in dreams.

Mirthful Melodies in December

Sing silly songs with a wobble and jig,
Tap dancing snowflakes all dressed in a gig.
Beats of the season, a humorous clash,
Dashing through jest like a wild, joyful dash.

With cocoa so hot, but the marshmallows fly,
An epic snowball, oh my, oh my!
Laughter erupts, like a fizzy delight,
As they launch their sweet treats into the night.

Funny faced snowmen stand guard by the door,
With noses all crooked and hats made of ore.
The air filled with chuckles, they twirl and they spin,
In the rhythm of glee, let the fun times begin!

Glowing Hearts and Giving Hands

Boxes of whimsy piled high at the door,
Each wrapped with a giggle, a chuckle, a roar.
Bright ribbons and bows in a jolly parade,
We unwrap the laughter, the silly cascade.

Hands making mischief, oh look at the mess,
What's hidden inside might just be a dress!
Yet under the chaos, the love starts to swell,
In every sweet moment, there's magic to tell.

With hugs and with tickles beneath the bright lights,
Sharing the joy that embraces our nights.
In every sweet gesture, our hearts play a tune,
A playful reminder that love's always strewn.

Luminous Spirits of Celebration

The lights are twinkling all around,
As laughter bounces off the ground.
We giggle as we trip on toys,
Unruly pets among the noise.

A jingle bell fell on my cat,
He thinks it's now the perfect hat.
Grandma slips on those rogue balloons,
And everyone bursts out in tunes.

The feast is set, but who can eat?
Between the chaos and the sweet.
A pie takes flight across the room,
While Uncle Fred sings just to zoom.

Tinsel-Touched Wishes upon the Breeze

The cold winds swirl with frosting bits,
Tinsel flies, oh what a blitz!
We toss snowballs that miss the mark,
Only to hit the neighbor's car.

Hot cocoa spills while friends just laugh,
We craft our snowmen with a gaffe.
One's got carrots, two left hands,
'He's perfect!' someone still demands.

A quiet night, but what a crew,
We dance around the grill, who knew?
A family feast with nailed-down chairs,
Oh, Auntie Sue and her wild flares!

Glimmering Dreams of Hearthside Gatherings

The fireplace crackles, oh so bright,
S'mores are sneaky in the night.
Kids run wild with sticky hands,
While Dad attempts his card game plans.

The puppy's snoozing on the mat,
While whispers float from every brat.
Grandpa's telling tales so tall,
We argue, 'Wait, that's not at all!'

The cookies hide, they're gone, oh dear,
Who ate the last one? Not me, I swear!
As laughter spills and stories fly,
Our hearts feel light, we're ready to cry.

Radiant Echoes of Frosty Fantasia

A snowflake landed on my nose,
And froze me up as laughter grows.
We see the world in shades of play,
As winter wonders come to stay.

From rooftops high, the snow falls down,
A slippery slide is our new crown.
A game of tag, we're cold and bold,
With cheeks so rosy, bright and gold.

With every cheer, the stories flood,
And mistletoe hangs where we stood.
We giggle at the tales retold,
In winter air, our hearts are gold.

Jingle Bell Whispers of Joy

Santa's sleighs go zooming fast,
Reindeer lined up, each one cast.
Elves are giggling, what a sight,
Wrapping gifts 'til late at night.

Cookies vanish in a flash,
Naughty kids make quite the splash.
Hot cocoa spills, a funny scene,
Slippers on, we jump and beam.

Snowmen wobble, hats askew,
Frosty faces join the crew.
Laughter echoes through the air,
Season's joy we love to share.

Chimneys smoke with roasted fun,
As carols blend, our hearts have won.
Twinkling lights and giggles cheer,
What a time of year, oh dear!

Winter's Festival of Glimmer and Glee

Sledding down the hills so steep,
Winter's magic makes us leap.
Snowball fights and frosty toes,
Everyone wears red, how it glows!

Mittens lost and scarves askew,
Chase a snowflake, me and you.
Fountains freeze, hot drinks in hand,
Jokes and puns across the land.

Icicles sparkle like a dream,
Warm laughter flows, a joyous stream.
Dancing lights, like fireflies,
Cheeks all rosy, what a prize!

Every corner filled with cheer,
Let's toast to a brand new year.
With goofy grins and happy cheer,
Together, we will persevere!

Frosted Delights Beneath the Mistletoe

Baking treats that rise and fall,
Flour flies, oh what a brawl!
Sugar sprinkles cover all,
A taste explosion at the ball.

Funny hats and jolly jumps,
Silly songs and happy thumps.
Charming smiles that shine so bright,
We dance around, what pure delight!

Gumdrop garlands grace the home,
Candy canes that love to roam.
Each a nibble, giggles near,
Every bite brings forth a cheer.

When the clock strikes merry time,
Join in laughter, rhyme and chime.
Memories made, we won't forget,
Mirth and fun, the best duet!

Harmonies of Honey and Hopes

Chiming bells in crisp, cold air,
Funny pranks are everywhere.
Sleigh rides taken, laughter rings,
Hopscotch made of winter flings.

With fuzzy socks, we prance around,
Wobble dance, we're homeward bound.
Mugs of cheerline every street,
Sugar highs that can't be beat.

Three-legged races, we go fast,
Losing track of time, what a blast!
Silly selfies, cheeks aglow,
Instants caught while we throw snow.

As evenings melt into delight,
Stories shared, a cozy night.
With joyous hearts, we find our way,
To celebrate this wondrous day.

The Joyful Chime of Giving Hearts

In a land where gnomes all dance,
They trip on gifts and laugh a chance.
A sleigh went flying, not a care,
With fruitcake flying through the air.

With twinkling lights on every tree,
The reindeer laugh so joyfully.
A penguin slid on ice so slick,
He tells a joke, then does a trick.

The snowmen wear the silliest hats,
They cluck like chickens, oh how they chat!
All gather round for a silly feast,
Finding giggles that never cease.

As laughter fills the frosty night,
Hearts grow warmer, spirits bright.
With every hug and silly grin,
This joyful time is where we begin.

A Kaleidoscope of Holiday Whimsy

In mistletoe jungles, kids explore,
With elves that squeak and snowflakes roar.
A carrot-nosed fellow sings out loud,
Wearing pajamas, so very proud.

The stockings hang with jump ropes inside,
A squirrel in a bowtie trying to hide.
A jellybean train runs off the track,
With giggling little guys in a snack attack.

With cookie dough snowballs in a race,
They fly through the air, what a messy place!
A dance-off with Santa, how silly to see,
He shows off moves from the '83.

Laughter erupts in every nook,
When Granny brings out her secret cookbook.
With shared smiles and playful cheer,
This whimsical season brings us near.

Sweet Serenades in Snow

As flakes come down like powdered sugar,
A reindeer strums a tune, quite a vugger.
Snowball fights with a musical twist,
You won't believe the fun you've missed!

A chorus of cats sings from the roof,
They tumble down, oh what a goof!
The gingerbread men dance on the ground,
In this frosty realm, joy is found.

A flamingo in a scarf takes flight,
While squirrels put on a circus tonight.
With every cheer and playful grin,
Sweet serenades begin to spin.

Hot cocoa flows like a bubbling brook,
As everyone shares their favorite book.
Through snowy nights, the laughter glows,
In these sweet moments, joy surely grows.

Jingle Bells and Gingerbread Dreams

In a baker's shop, flour clouds the air,
Frosting cascades with giggles to share.
A gumdrop mountain, sugary delights,
While marshmallow clouds float high on flights.

With candy canes swirling round and round,
A puppy in a bowtie leaps from the ground.
Tinsel twirls like a disco ball,
Jingo bells echo through the hall.

A wild parade of lollipops dance,
While peppermint penguins prance with a chance.
A circus of sweetness fills every room,
Laughter and joy in vibrant bloom.

As the clock strikes, the fun's not done,
With silly hats all ready for fun.
Together we sing with hearts so light,
In this merry world, everything's bright.

The Light of Kindness and Wonder

In a world of giggles, we roam,
With sweet delights that feel like home.
Laughing faces, sugar-coated dreams,
Sprinkling joy like magical beams.

Stockings hung with mischievous care,
Tinsel tangled in a dance so rare.
Elves chuckle, as snowflakes twirl,
In a whirlwind of fun, we unfurl.

Oh, the laughter, the playful tease,
Tickles and hugs bring instant ease.
With every chime, we skip and sway,
In the glow of kindness, we play.

Under the twinkling lights so bright,
We embrace the season, pure delight.
In silly hats, we jingle and prance,
Creating memories in our joyful dance.

A Glimpse of Glee in a Snowglobe

Inside a glass sphere, we take a ride,
Where snowmen giggle and penguins slide.
With tiny trees that seem to cheer,
It's a magical world, oh so dear.

A flick of the wrist, the snow starts to fall,
Tiny critters hop, having a ball.
With frosty noses and silly grins,
In this wintry realm, laughter begins.

Each shake of the globe brings joyous sights,
As candy-striped dreams twinkle like lights.
A scene full of whimsy, pure and bright,
Bringing warmth to the cold winter night.

Oh, how we marvel at this playful scene,
In moments like these, we feel so keen.
Collecting giggles, we spin with glee,
Lost in the wonder, just you and me.

Nostalgic Nibbles and Festive Friends

With plates of treats and laughter wide,
We gather 'round, with hearts open wide.
Stories shared, with nutty flare,
Each nibble brings us deeper care.

Frosted cookies, a touch of glee,
As messy hands craft a sweet jubilee.
Favors wrapped with ribbons and bows,
Each silly joke ignites the glow.

Old tunes playing, we clap and sway,
Reviving the spirits from yesterday.
In silly hats, we all would jest,
Creating moments that feel the best.

With love and mischief around the bends,
We toast to life with our trusty friends.
In this merry chaos, laughter blends,
As memories sweetly tie and mend.

Wondrous Nights Full of Magic

As stars twinkle in the night sky,
We hear jolly twang, a sonorous sigh.
The moon giggles, a mischievous glance,
Inviting us all for a playful dance.

With twirling snowflakes and frosty cheer,
We spin round, giggling, shedding fear.
The warmth of laughter rings through the night,
Turning cold moments into pure delight.

A gathering here where the fun unfolds,
With tales so funny, it's gold that molds.
We toast marshmallows under the stars,
While sharing the secrets of life and wonders.

Oh, wondrous nights, where magic soars,
In moments of joy, we open doors.
With every smile, we light up the dark,
Creating sparks that leave a mark.

A Symphony Wrapped in Ribbon

Bows on packages fly around,
Jokes and laughter are the sound.
Mittens tossed on snowy ground,
As giggles dance, joy is found.

Whiskers twitch on hungry pets,
Don't steal the treats, those are threats!
Sprinkled sugar, a clumsy mess,
Who knew that sweets would cause distress?

Chasing sprinkles with a broom,
Frosted chaos fills the room.
Lopsided hats and goofy grins,
As sugar highs turn to silly spins.

So lift your glass, cheer loud and clear,
To all the joy that brings us near.
Embrace the fun, let cares take flight,
In this wrapped mess, we find delight.

Sweets of the Season

Ribbons twist like tangled dreams,
Laughter erupts, or so it seems.
Gumdrop castles rise with bliss,
And who would trade this festive miss?

Frosting warriors armed with spoons,
Battling for crumbs like hungry goons.
Chocolate rivers flow with glee,
Watch out, that cookie's coming for thee!

The gingerbread house begins to sway,
A frosty breeze leads us astray.
Pretzel doors fly off the hinge,
This wacky feast makes us all cringe.

So wear that grin, embrace the mess,
In a whirlwind of sweetness, we are blessed.
Laughter rings through every bite,
In these moments, we feel so light.

The Dance of Dazzling Ornaments

Twinkling lights all over the place,
Ornaments skipping in wild grace.
Tinsel dangles, a shiny snare,
As cats plot schemes from their lair.

Wobbling bulbs on branches sway,
A delicate game, oh what a play!
With a plop, one drops from the tree,
"Wasn't me!" they shout with glee.

Silly faces made of fluff,
Ribbons pulled, oh that's enough!
Each bauble holds a story rare,
Together they glow without a care.

So spin and twirl, let laughter fly,
In this bouncy jolly sky.
With every sparkle shining bright,
Let's dance tonight, it feels so right.

Glistening Moments of Merriment

Snowflakes swirl with joyful cheer,
Wacky hats stretch from ear to ear.
Silly songs that go off-key,
Fill the air so joyfully.

Bowls of sweets pile up so high,
Sneaky fingers passing by.
With one quick swipe, it's all gone,
"Oh wait, let's sing that silly song!"

Chiming bells ring loud and proud,
Puffing cheeks in the crowd.
A pie stuck high on someone's head,
Through all this fun, we laugh instead.

So let your spirit leap and soar,
In a world where we laugh and roar.
With every moment, feel the light,
In the glow of joy, it's pure delight.

Glistening Moments of Yuletide Magic

Socks hung low, oh what a sight,
A mix of colors, oh so bright.
With sneaky nibbles, all in play,
Those treats will vanish by midday.

Jolly laughter fills the air,
As frosty air leads to a dare.
A slippery slide, who can resist?
The giggles echo, we've been kissed.

Twinkling lights dance on the tree,
Gifts wrapped tight, hidden with glee.
The puppy's tail wags in delight,
As he unwraps his new toy right.

Cookies crumble, tastes divine,
Sneaky fingers, a race to dine.
With every bite, a merry cheer,
Creating smiles, spreading the year.

Confections of Light in December's Glow

A sugar rush hits in the night,
As marshmallow fluff takes its flight.
Laughing at snowmen full of fluff,
Who knew making them could be tough?

Warming mugs, sweet scents arise,
Hot cocoa spills, oh what a surprise!
The snowflakes dance with sprightly glee,
As kids now race, will they get free?

Noses chilled, cheeks rosy bright,
Frosty faces in joyful plight.
An army of elves in mismatched socks,
Parading through streets, around the blocks.

Old sweaters worn, a cozy blend,
Sharing tales that will never end.
With giggles that sparkle, pure delight,
We sing through the chaos, the perfect night.

Festive Echoes of Merriment Unfolding

A whistle here, a bop right there,
Dance in circles, without a care.
The dog joins in with woofs and spins,
As laughter erupts, where fun begins.

Tinsel tangled, a comical sight,
As cats chase tails, adding to the fright.
The punch spills over, a vibrant hue,
Creating chaos, just like we do.

Surprises hidden in layers deep,
The giggles linger, can't help but peep.
Wrapped in stories, each moment shared,
Tickling fancies, none more scared.

With nutty jokes and playful jabs,
This season thrives on silly grabs.
As lights twinkle and friendships beam,
We lift our cups to our sweetest dream.

Lullabies of Laughter and Love

Hats askew and scarves all wild,
The snowball fight makes us feel like a child.
Giggles float on frosty air,
As snowflakes settle everywhere.

A choir of voices, off-key tunes,
With playful grins beneath the moons.
Each note a joke, each laugh a cheer,
It's not just a season; it's all we hold dear.

Tummy rumbles, what's in store?
A feast awaits, we'll soon explore.
With tiny bites, we munch with glee,
As we refill on warmth and giddy spree.

In cozy corners, stories flow,
Reminiscences of long ago.
With a wink and a nudge, laughter weaves,
Into hearts that build with love, a reprieve.

Seasons Greetings in Sugar Coating

Sugar plums dance on their tipsy toes,
As laughter bursts like frosty snow.
Chubby jolly elves, with cheeks so round,
Count every giggle, joyfully found.

Cocoa mugs clink with a playful cheer,
While sneaky squirrels steal desserts near.
Grandma's secret, a recipe twist,
Leaves us all in a sugary mist.

Holiday sweaters, bold and bright,
Spin like dreidels in winter light.
Snowflakes whisper with a giggling sound,
When mischief and delight abound.

Cookies crumble, a grand old affair,
As we all twirl in festive flair.
With each chomp, we can't help but grin,
For this sweet season, let the fun begin.

Festive Whispers in the Air

Tinsel twinkles like a sly cat's eye,
While chaos reigns, oh my, oh my!
Pretzels hang from the tree so proud,
As giggles echo, cheerful and loud.

Ornaments jingle, a playful sound,
While wobbly toddlers roll on the ground.
Jingle bells bounce on heads that sway,
As we dive headfirst into the fray.

Chorus of voices, off-key but bold,
Sing tales of mischief from years of old.
A dance party breaks out, all in a frenzied spin,
Like a merry-go-round where the laughs never thin.

Wrapping paper fights leave us all in a mess,
Bows on our heads, we feel quite the stress.
Yet with each laugh, we take to the air,
In moments of joy, we forget all our care.

Radiant Recollections of the Hearth

Fires crackle, and stories unfold,
With marshmallows roasted, a treat to behold.
Pajamas mismatched, socks from who knows,
Chasing each other, no one ever slows.

Great-uncles snore with a rhythmic sound,
While cousins conspire to sneak snacks around.
Board games explode with laughter and glee,
Overturned tables, oh what a spree!

Frosty windows with paintings of fun,
As we peek at the snowflakes, one by one.
Time for a snowball, who'll take the leap?
In this merry chaos, we find our keep.

Each snapshot a treasure, a giggly delight,
Of fuzzy sweaters and snowball fights.
These vibrant memories, spun from the air,
Whisper of joy shared, beyond compare.

Starry Skies and Snuggles

Under twinkling lights, we huddle so close,
Sharing sweet secrets, from the lightest to gross.
The moon winks down, a playful friend,
As we swaddle in warmth, our giggles extend.

A shadow appears, could it be Santa?
But it's just Uncle Joe, donning a bandana.
He trips on the cat, adding to the fun,
Laughter erupts, and the night's just begun.

Cookies and stories, each one a delight,
As we sip on warm cocoa, hearts feeling light.
A blanket of stars, a canopy so wide,
In this cozy moment, there's nowhere to hide.

With snowflakes a-falling like dreams from the sky,
We bundle together, as the hours fly by.
In snuggly embrace, we find peace and cheer,
Under twinkling stars, while the world disappears.

Cozy Corners and Heartfelt Tales

Beneath a warm blanket, in corners we nest,
Tales of old chuckles that made us feel blessed.
In mugs filled with warmth, on a chilly cold night,
We share belly laughs 'til we're all feeling bright.

The cat, in a sweater, is ready to pounce,
While stories take flight with each little bounce.
With mischief afoot, and misfits galore,
Our hearts grow together, like never before.

So gather around, let the giggles ignite,
We'll spin yarns of joy 'til the morning light.
For in cozy corners, love runs thick and wide,
With laughter unbridled, we've nothing to hide.

With heartfelt tales swirling, we cherish the past,
Each moment a treasure, let it forever last.
In this season of warmth, remember with glee,
The gift of good stories, just you and me.

Cinnamon Dreams and Sweet Nostalgia

The aroma of sweetness hangs thick in the air,
As gingerbread whispers come dance without care.
In this land of delight where the wild spices play,
We'll laugh until morning, it's just our own way.

With cookies and giggles, we pass time so slow,
Each smile brews magic, like hot cocoa flow.
The stories we share build a fortress of cheer,
In lovely old moments, we hold ever near.

As cinnamon spins tales of times that we miss,
Merriment lingers in moments like this.
Each crunch, each soft giggle, it warms like the sun,
In sweet nostalgia, we find we've won.

When laughter echoes with each sugary bite,
Through fragrant adventures, we find pure delight.
So here's to the memories, regardless of time,
For dreams filled with sweetness will forever chime.

A Waltz with Whipped Cream Clouds

In a kitchen full of giggles and cream,
Sugar sprinkles dance on a swirling dream.
With wobbly spoons and a chocolate fight,
We spin like tops 'til the morning light.

A frosty batch of mischief we make,
Fluffy clouds rise in sweet, frosty flakes.
Laughter explodes with each sticky fall,
As sprinkles rain down, we just cannot stall.

The oven's a monster, the timer's a joke,
Cookies are burning, and so is the smoke.
But who needs treats when we have this fun?
With frosting mustaches, we're surely all done.

In aprons so messy, we take a bow,
Grinning and giggling, we don't care how.
For in this sweet chaos, joy is the key,
Our waltz with cream clouds, the best jubilee!

Glowed Hearts Gathered in Kindness

Outside, the snowflakes shimmy and glide,
Inside, we're bundled, all snuggled and tied.
With mugs full of warmth, we toast to the night,
Gentle hearts whisper, 'Let's share this delight.'

A chorus of chuckles, a sprinkle of cheer,
As bright as the sparkles that dance in the air.
We chase little shadows that giggle and run,
In a game of pure joy, we've already won.

A quilt made of laughter, each patch sewn with care,
We gather around like a popsicle fair.
Stories grow wilder with each silly tale,
Under bright twinkling lights, we giggle and wail.

Embracing the warmth of our silly little crew,
We'll feast on our dreams, and maybe a stew.
So here's to our kindness, our hearts in the light,
With joy as our compass, we're always all right!

Nostalgic Whirls of Celebration

A dance through the years with a twist and a spin,
We chuckle at moments where silliness wins.
Old records are playing, a remix of fun,
As we laugh and we sway, feeling young while we run.

Bright tinsel and glimmer, the décor's a blast,
With pops of balloons as we echo the past.
A cake that's lopsided, but flavors so right,
Each bite brings us back like a silly delight.

The gifts might be riddled with giggles and glee,
Wrapped up with a ribbon that's stuck on a bee.
We jest about secrets and share all our dreams,
From mishaps to laugh tracks, we're bursting at seams.

So here's to the whirls that our hearts truly crave,
In a circle of friendship, so lively and brave.
With nostalgic vibes wrapped around us so tight,
We celebrate joyfully, from morning till night!

Lanterns of Laughter Shining Bright

In the glow of the lanterns, we gather around,
With voices a-chiming, sweet silliness found.
From tales of wild reindeer to snowman pranks,
Each chuckle's a lantern, our joy in big flanks.

A game of 'who's got the most mashed-up hat?'
With headwear of tinsel and a cat on the mat.
The giggles erupt like balloons in the air,
From all of the friends who congregate there.

With cookies on plates that are gnarled but adored,
We feast like the kings, with rumbles and roars.
In a world full of twinkles and jests on display,
Laughter's the language that brightens the way.

So let's dance beneath all the round, shining lights,
With lanterns of laughter empowering nights.
For in every heartbeat, joy lifts us up high,
And in this sweet moment, we reach for the sky!

Holiday Harmonies in the Frost

Snowflakes dance with glee,
Laughter rings from every tree.
A jolly elf with a red nose,
Sings off-key, but nobody knows.

Mistletoe hangs way too high,
A squirrel steals a piece of pie.
Yappy dogs in holiday hats,
Chasing shadows, plotting chats.

Chimneys puffing clouds of cheer,
While relatives linger near.
One uncle slips, oh what a sight,
Spilling cocoa, start a fight!

Twinkling lights and silly hats,
Uncles dance like clumsy cats.
With every chuckle, joy takes flight,
As laughter echoes through the night.

Sparkling Spirits of the Season

Jingle bells and goofy grins,
A cat jumps in, the mayhem begins.
Silly sweaters, loud and bright,
Grandma twirls, oh what a sight!

Frosty windows, slightly smeared,
A snowman winks, the kids all cheered.
Muffins burning, oh what fun,
The Great Cake Battle has begun!

Colorful treats piled high on days,
Sugar rush in a million ways.
Frosting fights in a gleeful spree,
As chaos reigns, just let it be!

Wrapping paper strewn around,
Joyful shouts and silly sounds.
With every smile, the spirits soar,
A sparkling season to adore!

Miracle Moments of Delight

Tiny hands with glue and cheer,
Making crafts to hang each year.
Mismatched socks, a silly scene,
A festive rainbow, bright and green.

Chubby cheeks and donut holes,
Watch the mischief, oh how it rolls!
A gift that wiggles, what could it be?
A dancing llama, can you see?

Sipping drinks that fizz and pop,
A two-headed snowman, let's not stop!
Giggles echo, joy on fire,
With every moment, hearts aspire.

Laughter lingers, hugs abound,
Magic found on playful ground.
In every corner, moments bloom,
A holiday filled with fun and zoom!

Joyful Gatherings in the Glow

A cat in a sweater purred with delight,
As mom tried to bake, but burned half the bite.
With sprinkles that flew from an accidental spill,
We laughed 'til we cried; what a glorious thrill!

The radio blared tunes from long, long ago,
While grandpa attempted to dance in the snow.
His two left feet made the whole room erupt,
As we cheered him on, with hot cocoa cupped.

Outside, the streetlights twinkled and glowed,
While the neighbors participated in the show.
With snowballs a-flying, the kids took a stand,
But poor little Timmy got hit with a hand!

In this wondrous moment, we joined a new game,
With laughter and stories, who could feel shame?
So here's to the memories, the hiccups, the cheer,
In gatherings warm, surrounded by dear.

Luminous Laughter and Twinkling Eyes

With socks mismatched and a giggle too loud,
A puppy was playing, engaging the crowd.
He chewed on the gift that was meant for the Dad,
And oh, how we laughed at the chaos he had!

The carrots for Rudolph got eaten with glee,
By Aunt Lucy, who claimed that they tasted like… tea?
With tea that was sweetened with sugar galore,
She danced 'round the room, wanting more and more!

Our sweaters were cozy, our hearts were so bright,
As we played goofy games under soft fairy light.
The mistletoe hung, a shy frog did leap,
And Uncle Bob kissed the cat, oh what a sweep!

The more that we laughed, the more that we shared,
Each story brought giggles, with moments declared.
For among all the sparkle and joy that resides,
Are luminous laughter and love that abides!

Marshmallow Dreams on Frosty Nights

With snowflakes a-swirling, the night felt so grand,
A snowman insisted we take a firm stand.
He wore a top hat, but missed his sharp nose,
Claiming the carrot was too big, goodness knows!

As cocoa was sipped and marshmallows flew,
The fun found a way to twirl and construe.
With bubbles of laughter that filled all the space,
We feigned we were serious but couldn't keep face!

Then a carol-off started, a battle of sorts,
With voices so silly, we felt like good sports.
We each took a turn, trying to outshine,
But grandpa serenaded as his voice went divine!

So here we will stay, in this jolly delight,
With marshmallow dreams and hearts oh so light.
For each frosty evening that brings us together,
Creates cherished moments, through all sorts of weather!